Cypherpunk visions and trends 2023-2025

JURAJ BEDNÁR

Written in 2023 (with few notes in 2024) by Juraj Bednár
I don't care about copyrights.

Be excellent to each other and enjoy the book!

Table of contents

Introduction

We are coming out of a pandemic into turmoil and increased volatility. War in Ukraine led to (an addition to murdering innocent people) changing perceptions of world power. Formerly emerging countries want a seat at a table. Regulators are crazy, regulating everything from charging ports, artificial intelligence to cryptocurrencies and messaging apps. We can only laugh at the past madness of mandatory cookie boxes on websites and other nonsense. What is coming from them is way worse.

Metaphorical money printers were working non-stop during the pandemic and as I write this at the beginning of 2023, we experience monetary deflation, but we are already far beyond any reasonable monetary expansion. The inflation will slowly melt and create Cantillon effect islands of inflation that will hurt the most and enrich the few.

We cypherpunks have a unique worldview. We do not strive to change the world for the masses and definitely not for everyone. We believe that we can use technological tools to improve our lives, but we do not try to force them on anyone.

This is a positive book, even though it does not start like one. Why?

In this short book, I want to present you with the visions, trends and wishes **for cypherpunks**, not for the general population. These technologies will (hopefully) appear or improve in the following years. They can be used by anyone, but they will not be used by everyone. Some people still believe in the old-world-order, in politicians, parliaments, commissions and top-down hierarchical models of governing society.

Cypherpunks are striving to be ungovernable, hidden. We do not concern ourselves with things like "how can an average employee with a mortgage make use of this?" We aim to not be an average employee with a mortgage in the first place.

In short - we want to plant flowers and trees. For us, they are in the form of technologies, tools or even different mindsets.

This book aims to plant a few seeds and help them grow. For technological creators, the goal is to give them entrepreneurial ideas. For cypherpunks (the clients of these entrepreneurs), it should describe what tools to look for, to create demand for them and help them find ways to solve problems that are likely to arise in the future.

Many of these solutions already exist - from peer to peer OTC bitcoin markets, proxy merchants, privacy tools to sovereign open-source artificial intelligence and decentralized energy production. We hope that we start using them more, seeing their potential and a way to improve our lives.

Cypherpunk technologies power cryptoanarchist philosophy and create practical tools to solve common problems, such as systematic breaking of natural rights, censorship, violence, theft. These tools improve human cooperation, help peer to peer societal structures and enable more ways to enjoy our lives and sow the fruits of our labor. But first, we must plant some flowers and trees

Let's dive in…

Deregulation as competitive advantage, jurisdictional arbitrage

As regulations are introduced, many people try to avoid them. This trend is not new. Some novel stem cell therapies are done in Panama instead of the USA (where they were pioneered). Even Tony Robbins writes about it and promotes it. The philosophy of jurisdictional arbitrage "go where you are treated best" sums it up the best. As you will see throughout this book, it is important to understand several threads of development. On one hand, countries compete for business and introduce new loopholes to attract capital, on the other hand, everything gets more difficult. Dubai introduced several regulations including income tax (although not in Free Zones), Paraguay made it more difficult to obtain permanent residency (you need to go through temporary residency and additional bureaucracy) and more countries are joining reporting cartels with OECD-introduced Common Reporting Standard.

On the other hand, cypherpunk technologies enable true globalization. Some profitable companies do not even need a legal entity or jurisdiction and are powered by technologies. Dark Fi introduced the concept of AnonDAO, where the members of the DAO (decentralized autonomous organization), their votes and stakes are anonymized using zero knowledge technologies, homomorphic encryption, and other technologies.

People still have options to escape regulatory hells and on top of that, we have ever improving technologies of societal organization – with interactions, governance and capital – that allow for privacy-preserving cooperation.

I have written a paper about deregulation as a key driver of post-covid economic recovery[1]. Deregulation is key for states to survive and attract capital (including people). For us individuals, we can ride this trend and go where we are treated best for a specific purpose (spending, making money, incorporating, banking, …). The principle of jurisdictional arbitrage and its profitability means that we will never have one regulatory hell, but competing jurisdictions. That does not mean we should become fans of any particular state - the regulations change all the time and what was once a good country becomes a regulatory hell.

As my friend Pavol Luptak says, the best way to take advantage of jurisdictional arbitrage is becoming global and flexible. A country introduced a regulation that impacts your business? Goodbye country A, we go to country B. People often say you cannot pick cherries from the top. Sure we can! And we should!

That is why Pavol Luptak and I founded a company called Liberation Travel. It helps cypherpunks decentralize and make use of these jurisdictional arbitrage opportunities - with permanent residencies, plan Bs (plural) and introducing flexibility into our lives.

---

[1] Juraj Bednár: Post-COVID Economic Recovery: Innovation, Investment, Deregulation, 2022

New lifestyles - van nomadism, perpetual travel, digital nomads and vonu

Being global, flexible and making use of jurisdictional arbitrage brings another positive side effect. Many forms of state harassment disappear if the state thinks you are a tourist, or a nomad. Often you need to register or even ask for permission to stay somewhere more than a certain time (30 to 90 days is common length of stay for tourist visas in many countries). After more than a half year somewhere, tax residency kicks in and you are supposed to pay local taxes. Of course you "should not work" on tourist visas. As people become stationary, they are tied to a land, which is the perfect condition in which states start harassing you and milking you for tax revenue.

One of the most interesting (and unknown!) libertarian practices that reduce harassment is called "vonu". The Vonu podcast website (I highly recommend the podcast!) defines vonu as *"the condition or quality of, as well as the action of achieving, an invulnerability to coercion"*.

There are many definitions of freedom. I like the definition of optionality and positive liberty, which is also a direct guide to increasing your freedom. If you optimize for increased options and creative output, you do not have "freedom from" something, but you increase a positive "freedom to". If you are free, what do you do with your freedom? That's why I emphasize creative output (which can be approximated by profit, but beware who you talk to, profit does not have a good rep among mainstream "servile society").

Vonu on the other hand optimizes for "freedom from" and I think it is one of the best ways to optimize this type of negatively defined freedom (negatively not in a form of negative emotion, but a strategy to avoid something - in this case harassment). The goal of vonu is to attain the longest mean time to harassment - how many months or years till you have to fill a form, ask for permission or fight some kind of enforcement.

There are many ways to escape this - on the extreme side would be escaping into the jungle and not interacting with people whatsoever. But there are other options, such as van nomadism. If you are traveling across the world, you get a lot of benefits of a nomad lifestyle that have worked for millenia. People working the soil on the farms were often taxed, counted (and put in a government database), and milked for revenue and work. They became members of the servile society (again from Vonu podcast: "*a society that does not respect self-ownership or individual liberty, but rather heralds the supremacy of government and authority; in other words, it upholds the collective as superior to the individual*"). On the other hand, people without the "benefits" of the land were often free(er). No one wanted to bother with them and waste time with them, if they knew they would be gone in a few weeks or months and the expected revenue out of them is maximized by letting them spend their money voluntarily rather than taxing them.

This is on one hand based on the fact that it becomes quite difficult to differentiate among tourists and potential taxpayers, but also countries that would harass tourists would see them turning away and going elsewhere. If revenue from tourism is important for a country, they like to treat them nice - often nicer than the local population.

Digital nomadism has been a hip way of achieving this. Many people do remote work for an employer, but increasingly, people work outside of employer-based corporate hierarchies - they switched to node-first networks as solopreneurs, entrepreneurs or even hustlers. A company of one, interacting with others and using communication technologies to produce and deliver the results, is one of the best ways to make a living for cypherpunks. If the payment for these services is in cryptocurrencies, you are achieving even better outcomes for yourself, you are using global non-inflationary money.

Many people would object that this kind of lifestyle is not for everyone, some people like their office job, or need to be physically present somewhere rather than roam around the world. This objection is true, but remember we are **not looking** for solutions for **everyone**. A majority of the population would not want to live like this, but we are not a majority. On the other hand, we are not born with a single career. Something that might not have been for us can suddenly become our best option, but it might change the way we make a living.

Another option is van nomadism. This allows us to reduce transaction costs of setting up accommodation by taking our homes with us. Van nomadism was described by Rayo, who invented Vonu, as a way to increase mean time to harassment. Before anyone is interested in you, you leave. Digital nomadism is a more contemporary concept that has been greatly expanded during the pandemic - people realized that they do not need to do their work from their office, so why not go to a better city, or a better country? Better might be a better climate, cheaper living conditions or simply a country where it is nice to live. Working with New York or London based company (or better a extra-jurisdictional DAO) does not have to mean you can't look at sunsets of Chiang Mai, Thailand.

Perpetual travelers do this in a way where they move to a different country often enough not to be considered a tax resident of any country (but beware of some local regulations that might make this harder).

Often, when I talk to people about these lifestyles, they think it is an obscure way of life for hippies and I am not mainstream enough. Some even go as far as thinking we are crazy. Looking at some numbers, we can see that there are at least 35 million digital nomads. Interesting facts from the study:

- If the global digital nomad community were a country, it would rank #41 by population size, just after Canada (37,742,154) and Morocco (36,910,560) in population size (Source: ABrotherAbroad.com)
- If the global digital nomad community were a country, it would be 38th most prosperous country based on gross national income per capita, ranking just after Portugal ($23,200 average annual income per person) and Saudi Arabia ($22,840 average annual income per person) (Source: ABrotherAbroad.com)
- The average digital nomad has a higher monthly budget than the average income of citizens from the top 5 countries digital nomads prefer to nomad, and 9 of the top 10 countries for digital nomads (Source: ABrotherAbroad.com)

This means that this is not an obscure minority that can be easily discarded. These people are usually wealthier than the average citizen that has not left. They are very probably wealthier than the average population in the countries that they live in. This means they can spend their money and support local economies, becoming a wealth improving force for many people. This is why they are usually welcome even by countries that are otherwise hostile even to their own citizens.

Van life, digital nomadism, perpetual travel and vonu are among the few strategies that increase mean time to harassment in the "meatspace" (also called "real world"). The strategy could be best described as a metaphor of always being a tourist everywhere you are, but for the country that gave you your passport, you are a homeless expat abroad that lives off debt.

We might see many interesting new ways of living. Internet connectivity is abundant and the rise of parallel (and cypherpunk) economies enables making a living using global digital currencies and digital communication technologies, plus (hopefully recovering well after pandemic) logistics and travel networks.

Anonymity engineering and AnonDAO

Privacy-preserving cooperation is part of a cryptoanarchist program laid out by Timothy C. May in his Cryptoanarchist manifesto. It requires anonymous communication, including financial communication. In anonymity engineering (a term coined by Amir Taaki who is working on DarkFi), the developers are combining privacy primitives to compose applications. It is a different approach then traditional algorithmic (computational) approach, although it uses standard programming languages - but also creating new languages that allows composing of these privacy-preserving building blocks. Instead of recording the sending X amount of a cryptocurrency, you create a zero-knowledge proof that outputs of the transactions are lower than inputs, proving to everyone that the sender of the transaction did not spend more than they had. Instead of recording votes in a DAO, you compose proofs that the voting happened according to rules and the result is valid.

While AnonDAO and anonymity engineering is in its infancy (dark.fi did not yet launch mainnet implementation), this sort of novel thinking is important for cypherpunks and it creates a lot of opportunities. Not only in business, but in culture and philosophy. As anyone with a social network account knows, anonymity often brings out the worst in people. What if these people could control money flows? Of course they have something that anonymous social network accounts do not have – skin in the game (voting is based on some sort of merit or stake in a project). Will these projects be for good or will they be glorified over-engineered troll farms?

I hope for a more positive outcome, but it will not happen by itself – we must shape it into this form. If someone wants to do something interesting that has not been done before, this is one of the most interesting areas in the following years.

One of the first concrete examples of these principles is the founding of LunarDAO - an organization that helps create these privacy preserving technologies. The people behind this project are pseudonymous and we will see what kind of cooperation this brings and what the results will be. It is certainly something that has not been tried enough. Probably the only other example that comes to my mind is Bitcoin itself, which was created by a pseudonymous author (or group of authors?) and created a structure of social interaction in addition to a new parallel monetary system. This way of creation led to a structure that removed hierarchy (there is no "Bitcoin CEO"), but it did not avoid politics entirely. What remains to be seen is - if an organization can be started by the community with pseudonymous members, voting is anonymous (and merit-based) and discussions are pseudonymous, will they be able to avoid the trap of politics? Removing hierarchy is the necessary first step.

Anonymity and privacy are essential for the operation of arbitrage outside of old-world jurisdictions (states). If we truly want to interact outside of primate hierarchical structures and move into a post-primate world (see Paul Rosenberg's book Post Primate Society), we need to move our communication out of the control of the hands of the rulers.

The main primitives (cryptocurrencies, end-to-end
encrypted communication) are in place. The
renaissance of anonymity engineering will bring
even more tools (such as AnonDAO) and by using
these tools to create non-hierarchical societal
structures, we might find ourselves at the
forefront of post-primate parallel societies.

Parallel societies

Many people are not happy. Many areas of human production are completely taken over by the state(s) to the liking of corporations, in an arrangement we call "crony capitalism". Take this book as an example. If I wanted to sell it to you peer to peer, I would have to find where you are (some countries require recording of two to three "proofs" of residence), calculate and charge you the proper VAT/sales tax rate. While there are plug-ins for eshops that make all this hell bearable, filing tax declarations in countries most people have never heard of is not as much fun. Yes, if you are an author from Paraguay and you want to sell the book to someone in Romania, you have to charge them Romanian VAT, declare it and then wire the money to Romania. What if someone buys from South Korea? Or the U.S. state of Georgia?

Of course, this is all easy if I sell through Amazon – they deal with all this bureaucracy and after withholding taxes, pay me 20%-30% of the sale price of the book.

How many people will say "screw it" and just do all this in a parallel economy, with parallel money? Increasingly more and more people. Selling produce through real-world social networks, voluntary energy and food exchange markets will probably become more common. I think even peer to peer medicine markets after shortages of basic OTC medicine in countries with socialist healthcare systems (almost all of the world by now) will become more common. Pharmacy does not have ibuprofen? Maybe this "darknet" market has some. And I am not even making it up, although "darknet" in this case are clearnet classified sites. Yes, rockets fly to space almost every day now, and yet pharmacies sometimes do not have ibuprofen.

For more information on parallel economies, see my blog Shorting the state – how to benefit from parallel solutions and competition with the state and of course a chapter on Parallel economies and why they work in Cryptocurrencies – Hack your way to a better life.

Cryptocurrencies as a parallel financial system

Among the main parallel economies are financial and money markets and healthcare. Increasing number of people have negative experiences with the traditional financial system, so let's have a closer look at it. It starts with ever-inflating money supply causing the increase of prices, Cantillon effect and resulting decrease of wealth and quality of life.

Volatility wins over stability

The major complaint about cryptocurrencies used to be volatility. Truth being told, most cryptocurrencies are not just volatile, they go to zero. We have many such examples, while counterexamples are scarce – Bitcoin, Monero, Ethereum and a few more. I am not a Bitcoin maximalist, but let's consider Bitcoin for now. It has been volatile and it dropped from its all time high to less than 30%. On the other hand, we have almost certainty of debasing fiat currencies.

Many people will realize that volatility is something that can be handled with various strategies, but a sure and planned ("inflation target") ride towards zero of fiat currencies is more problematic. Of course you can make use of both of these effects by shorting fiat currencies with Bitcoin collateral (I have a course how to do it and I describe other strategies for volatility in my book Cryptocurrencies – Hack your way to a better life).

Unexpected volatility is a problem, but can we realistically say that crypto's volatility is unexpected? And if it is expected, we should act accordingly and change our strategies, not deny reality.

Of course, this is also a mindset thing. Or – if you change your mindset, you suddenly can see ways to operate despite volatility, or even using it for your benefit (again, I recommend at least the Bitcoin strategies chapter of Cryptocurrencies – Hack your way to a better life).

Financial transactions and accessibility of money

Lately, people are learning that their money is not their money. A cool hacker project called Flipper Zero had their account frozen by PayPal, with $1.3 million of funds sent by customers as payment for their orders. Quite insane - the service that should allow you to get paid freezes your money, leaving people without the product and without their money.

Many people who were born with a bad passport do not have access to financial services. And yet there are many people who do not have a passport at all. For all these people, financial services are completely inaccessible.

There are many people who have bank accounts and think that their money in the bank is really their money. They believe that when they send a transaction from the bank's web or mobile interface, the transaction will go through. The cases where it does not even get sent or does not arrive to the recipient are occurring with increasing frequency.

This belief is increasingly shattered to pieces.
Many people who entered the parallel and crypto
economies did so because a bank suddenly closed
their account, or they were not able to use it for
the transaction they wanted to do.

Unbanked people know they are unbanked.
Banked people do not know that banks (mostly
thanks to regulations) are more broken every year.
The number of banked people with a bad
experience will grow. And the solutions for the
unbanked will probably also work for the *banked,
but pissed'* category.

The rise of lunarpunk

I have written about lunarpunk in my book and the chapter is also published on my blog – "Lunarpunk – the future of cryptocurrencies in regulatory hell". Lunarpunk is a response to the inevitable state attack on privacy technologies and cypherpunk projects. As the need for states, corporations, and criminal groups to monitor, tax, regulate, and surveil increases, a natural response arises – a technology of anonymity, encryption, invisible unregulated financial flows, and other forms of communication is and further will be developed and used by the people. With such positive feedback loop, the need to regulate and monitor is again reinforced ("see, they are avoiding our control, we need to increase surveillance!"), thus improving technologies to circumvent regulation and surveillance even more.

Lunarpunk predicts that this conflict fuels the creation of privacy and anonymity technology that is antifragile to state attacks – all other projects that cannot sustain these attacks die out and their users move to the surviving projects, further fueling their growth.

Lunarpunk is a new ideology, but it is based in real projects that have privacy and user empowerment as basic building blocks.

While anonymity engineering is the technology that powers these new privacy preserving and user empowering technologies, lunarpunk describes the general market dynamics. To win (and be profitable), you first need to survive. And those that do not survive fertilize the soil for those that do.

As the states try to regulate more parts of private life and contaminate societies with their dominance hierarchies, we avoid this by building tools – *the dark forest, lit by the moon.* The dark forest is the environment of diverse privacy tools that allows users to keep their matters private, but let them communicate, exchange and create.

Don't forget to watch "lunarpunk primer" by rekt.news and Rachel Rose O'Leary. It was the best video I've seen in 2022.

Progressive web apps and desktop app renaissance

People moved from desktop computers to smartphones, which are dominated by two platforms and their "stores" – Google Play Store and Apple App Store. These stores try to protect users by disallowing malware, but to achieve that, they are regulated and control what can be listed and sold through them. They also regulate how payments are processed (to force app publishers to pay the "Google and Apple tax" – a percentage for processed payments).

Imagine you are an author of a Free and Open Source software (FOSS), and some insane country creates a regulation against encryption, or anonymous cryptocurrencies. Of course, your software is FOSS, so you do not care, but this regulation will be enforced by the stores.

As someone who has published an app in these stores, I have to say that these regulations are always changing, apps get rejected (even just new app versions that release a bugfix!) because of some new item in terms and conditions, or a tax in some country you have never heard of.

Therefore, I expect many more Progressive Web Apps (PWAs) to appear and be used by an increasing number of projects and people. PWA is a new concept of a web application that acts like a smartphone app. You can add it to the home screen. And you do not have to use a platform's official store app.

PWAs can have a look and feel like a native app, even use some advanced technologies (such as NFC, scanning QR codes, location, if you allow it, uploading files, access to photos, etc.). These technologies allow for apps that are permissionless.

As more regulations on encryption, privacy technologies (such as Monero) and exchanges are in force and as Apple and Google become hungrier for the fees, and more servile to the states, these kinds of apps will make more sense and will empower the users.

Then there are desktop apps. They do not have to rely on the not-so-privacy-minded bloatware of a web browser and can be built to run on laptops. No data needs to be sent to servers, communication can be peer to peer, or apps can work offline. These apps often have a bit worse user interface, but they can empower users by allowing them to do more. And if the software is FOSS, everyone can improve it.

No-code and low-code apps

With the advent of chat-controlled AI systems such as ChatGPT, more people can write code using these assistants. This will increase the pace of learning programming for some, and create a fog of cluelessness for many others that 'write code' by searching for answers on stackoverflow.com or now using ChatGPT. I think that knowledge of programming is one of the most useful skills you can have in this time as a human, but let's empower also the people who cannot code. That is why I am bullish on no-code tools.

No-code tools enable creation of applications (usually web apps) without writing code. That does not mean it is necessarily easy – in the same way I cannot use professional 3D modeling tools or even 2D graphics editing tools such as Photoshop or GIMP. Even though they do not require coding, you need to know what you are doing – what do all the settings and filters do, etc.

With no-code tools, you can create applications without coding, but you need to know how to use these tools. They might be easy, such as spreadsheets or presentation software. I have seen amazing apps written as an "excel sheet". Not everything needs to be done in the coolest programming language (talking about you, Go, Rust and Python!).

I believe this started with tools such as Wordpress. Before Wordpress, people were writing custom HTML/CSS code for every website. Some people were even programming their own „content management systems". I personally wrote at least a few and used at least a dozen of them. They required knowledge of coding, or at least using their templating engines.

WordPress democratized and demonetized the creation of websites. Because it is Free and Open Source Software, anyone can use it and host the resulting website themselves or with one of literally thousands of providers. What took thousands of dollars and months of web-designers' effort is now literally a one man job for a few afternoons that an average coffee shop owner can do themselves. With the use of plug-ins, Wordpress allows you to create e-shops, learning portals or other more complex applications by installing either free or paid plug-ins. And there are no coding requirements.

Unfortunately, there is not a WordPress plug-in for everything (although more than a few people would dispute this statement) and there are really some custom applications out there.

That's why I like to look at tools such as Bubble.io, Carrd.co, Notion.so, Airtable or Budibase.com. They allow creating simple or even more complex apps, connected to a database, interacting with other systems, etc. Many of these are Software as a Service and make you depend on a third party, which is not permissionless, encrypted, anonymous and usually does not integrate well with parallel economy (through encrypted communication and cryptocurrencies). Out of the above, Budibase is Free and Open Source Software and can be run on your own infrastructure.

Even cypherpunks who cannot code can develop some software, which if proven useful can be then improved, or even rewritten by professional programmers. Because cryptoanarchy is a decentralized movement, we desperately need experiments, that is a major way how we improve. Centralized solutions improve by incremental tinkering with an occasional newcomer disrupting the market and taking users over to their solution. Failures are often fatal to the whole ecosystem. Decentralized and smaller markets need frequent newcomers. Users can rapidly switch to a better solution and often take their data with them (thanks to the open-source philosophy).

I hope no-code tools will enable more experimentation.

Open-source artificial intelligence

Probably everyone has played with tools such as ChatGPT, Midjourney, Stable Diffusion, or DALL-E. Some people tried Github's Copilot (a programmer's assistant). I used Midjourney to create all the images in this book, including the cover. I use AI tools to fine-tune the sound of my podcast, translate my books and articles, etc.

There are many of these amazing tools that empower the users, make their lives easier and help them in being more productive. I used to brag that I am 10x more productive than the average person just because I can write code and automate many tasks that people struggle with manually. Now, people will be as productive as me, if they adopt these tools.

There's one problem though. ChatGPT is very biased in its worldview. Ask it about Bitcoin or morality of paying taxes and you realize that it has learned not from the best in the field, but from the majority. And the majority is dull, boring and often wrong. Ask Midjourney to draw something controversial and it will refuse. But if you look at Stable Diffusion, you realize that removing this filter is literally about commenting out three lines of code in its source code. Yes, the difference is that Stable Diffusion is open-source.

Of course, I understand that there is an enormous cost in training these models and some non-trivial cost in running them. There are some things we want to do with these tools that we are not too eager to upload to some third-party cloud service for processing. I used to work in a very secretive field of computer science and there were things that we never wrote in an online Google document, even though the user interface and usability of Google workspace was more than enough, and it would have enabled easy online collaboration. There are open-source tools for that now – such as NextCloud, or the note taking app Standard Notes. I think the same will inevitably happen in various AI fields, although it might take a bit longer.

Training a model like ChatGPT can cost tens to hundreds of millions of dollars. Ray Kurzweil said that current doubling rate of the number of trained parameters in neural networks is six months ("original" Moore's law is 18 months doubling of computational power). While we play with ChatGPT or Stable Diffusion, someone is already testing a trained model that is twice as powerful. This of course comes down to increasing investments, but also optimizing the training and gathering of the data for the training set.

While open source conversational models exist, they are not nearly as impressive as ChatGPT yet – more like GPT-2 (a predecessor to GPT-3, which is the basis of ChatGPT) level. What is important is that the research and training of these models in a true open-source fashion is happening.

As a person who likes to be productive, I would like to let AI handle my emails or let it write some things for me (like replies to bureaucrats – public or private). As a cypherpunk though, I did not spend my energy migrating to end-to-end encrypted platforms, just to hand over my communication and my intentions to some cloud based AI platform; however nice their privacy policy might be (hint: it is not nice).

Also, I would like to be able to "up-train" my model. I don't want my AI say things I do not believe. My personal AI should know what I think. It should learn from the books I've read and liked. Mainstream, average person (which does not exist in reality!) has mainstream dull opinions. We are unique and we need to teach the AI that we use some of that uniqueness ourselves. A medical doctor's "personal AI" should not talk like lifestyle magazine pop-med articles, and a cypherpunk's AI should have a proper argument on immorality of coercion.

I sincerely hope we will get there sooner rather than later. Possibilities are endless, but we must be in control.

Note from 2024: This is happening and I am part of it. I fine-tuned my JurAI model, even on the content of this book. Find it on Nostr.

Regulation-free peer to peer over the counter exchange between crypto and fiat

The story is always the same. We've seen it in Colombia, Nigeria, Vietnam, and many other countries. Institutional exchanges get regulated by the state, or banks and a thriving over the counter peer to peer market appears. It started with sites such as localbitcoins and localmonero. Of course, peer to peer trades among persons usually do not follow what are now standard institutional KYC procedures. Therefore, states sometimes attack these marketplaces (localbitcoins has since introduced KYC). The reasons for attacks are not important, what is important to realize is that every regulation creates a thriving parallel economy, where trades are truly peer to peer. These trades are often not regulated, but even if they are, the compliance of peer to peer OTC with regulations is very low.

Thriving P2P OTC markets enable "undocumented" people (i.e. people to whom the government refused to print an ID) to buy and sell cryptocurrencies and enable anonymous access to the crypto economy to others.

I have written a blog on bootstraping an OTC market in your town, among your friends and acquaintances (also a chapter in Cryptocurrencies – Hack your way to a better life).

Why is it important and why does it work? Let's first consider how these trades work in a hypothetical completely regulated environment. A good way to think about it is thinking how people buy weed on markets where weed sales are prohibited. A person that wants to buy weed asks around their social network – a classmate who was already a pothead in high school. Maybe they stopped smoking, but they know who still sells some weed. It usually takes less than twelve hours from the moment someone wants to smoke until someone has a joint in their hand, ready to light it up.

This works for several reasons. The social "link" carries implicit information of "I know this guy, he's definitely not a cop" (sometimes this information is even explicitly verified). Also, weed is something so common everywhere in the world that the property of small world networks will get you a connection in the social graph fast (so called "Six degrees of separation"). It works even for more exotic things (a special screw for a tractor for example), but the more common it is, the easier it is to get to a person who can solve a particular problem.

The social graph grows exponentially if you add "hops" in the network (friends, friends-of-friends, friends-of-friends-of-friends). Of course, not everyone who would find a connection will actually help and ask around. Fortunately, even with low compliance of requests, you will probably get what you want soon.

This effect is not used by many online marketplaces such as localbitcoins – there is no social graph and no apparent reputation through social graph. These portals often have a reputation system, but it is based on previous trades. This type of reputation is prone to sibyl attacks. As the number of regulations grows, and so does the crypto economy, more people will realize that being a P2P OTC trader and solving this problem for others is a good (side) business (this is not a business recommendation, always make sure you won't end up in jail or worse!).

But this is now; what is the future? There are projects such as Vexl. This project aims to automate this discovery process. The social connections are followed in a (semi-)automated way by using a contact list and combining it with user-specified location (to do in-person trades in a particular city, not GPS-based position). If the connection that you find is not direct (a friend you have directly in the contact list), you can ask a common contact if the person you want to trade with is trustworthy. Vexl is being tested in the Czech Republic and Slovakia as I write these lines, but should launch soon on the international market. What makes it unique is that Vexl does not see the offers directly and does not facilitate the trade.

It is a social graph exploring tool – you need to meet (preferably in person) and do the trade yourself, Vexl does not touch the money.

I mentioned the Lunarpunk video above, Vexl has the second best video of 2022, be sure to watch it too!

Proxy merchants become more important

Proxy merchants are people who facilitate trades between two markets that cannot communicate directly. Imagine that cryptocurrencies are banned completely and everyone is forced to trade using governments' Central Bank Digital Currencies (CBDCs). Many people would call this the end of crypto, but I think it just signals the rise of opportunities for proxy merchants to solve this problem. Say you want to buy a car or a house. A proxy merchant is someone who has the necessary structure to make it happen. You pay them in crypto, they pay for your house or car. It might be in the form of selling you an offshore company that owns the property (thus using different rules - a change in another government's database), or something similar.

If there are people who have money in the form of cryptocurrencies and things they want to buy, there are people who are willing to solve this problem for them, for a fee.

Proxy merchants do also the opposite kind of trade – there are many opportunities in crypto economies, such as earning a fiat interest rate in DeFi or using Bitcoin futures (see Cryptocurrencies book). These opportunities are not accessible to people without crypto knowledge (think older relatives) and can be made available through proxy merchants.

I consider services that enable access to the traditional economy, such as sellers of gift cards (Bitrefill, Coincards), among proxy merchants. They are a bit difficult, because they are normal regulated businesses, yet they are building a bridge between crypto economy and traditional economy without KYC (this is key). Let's say you want to top up your prepaid data plan or buy something on Amazon. You pay these services in crypto and they facilitate the exchange – either top up your plan directly or sell you a gift card that you can apply and use. It is a way to sell crypto for fiat-denominated payment methods (such as Amazon gift cards).

Describing all kinds of proxy merchants is difficult, because they must react to the local regulatory environments and will have to solve the problems that we cannot foresee yet. One thing is for sure – if there's money to be made, someone will do it and solve this problem for us. That is why I do not fear crypto regulations.

New social networks

Cypherpunk social networks have been different from traditional ways of communication since the beginning of cypherpunk ideas. Communicating through Internet Relay Chat (IRC) using just nicknames, being friends with people you've never seen and do not know their "legal name" was common for us. We were communicating in groups ("channels") that were based on topics. It is a similar experience to Slack or Discord, but with a different vibe, that changes the quality of discussion. On cypherpunk networks, there is no censorship, there is often encryption and pseudonymity or anonymity is expected.

We are moving from old-school big tech social networks (Facebook, Twitter, Instagram) towards private groups on Signal, Element/Matrix, SimpleX or DarkFi's peer to peer IRC. There are experiments such as status.im that try to combine functioning of DAOs with tokens and social networks. For example, only a person with some amount of token or holding a type of NFT can enter a room. Voting and other features are expected in future versions.

I have discussed the need for end-to-end
encrypted chat applications and written a
comparison of current projects in the
Cryptocurrencies book, but also published them
online for free. I believe this industry will grow.
There are new projects with different approaches
coming up all the time.

These technologies will be the technological basis
powering ideas such as The Network State by
Balaji Srinivasan.

Interactions in groups are not the only use of
social networks. We often use social networks also
as a public square, mainly for promoting our
products and services, building brands, etc. I
know it has a bad rep, but you also needed a way
to learn about this book. Have you heard about it
in a podcast or followed me or someone who liked
it and wrote about it on Twitter? One way or
another, you need to learn about these things
somehow. Creating something that has no users,
no customers and no readers is wasting time. Of
course promoting these things in closed Signal
groups is useful, but sometimes a more public
approach is needed.

Twitter, Facebook and Instagram have "the algorithm" (for a nice philosophical description, be sure to follow the ideas of Alexander Bard). "The algorithm" is part of the programming of social networks that chooses which posts from the thousands of available posts you are seeing. The big tech social networks have been criticized for optimizing for engagement, which often means negativity, conflict, and polarization. I am not sure if "the algorithm" is the cause of the polarization of society and I do not think that this polarization is only negative. Cypherpunks have long been at the edge of society and in conflict on values with violent statist philosophies all along. The fact is that we do not have control over the algorithm. We can think we can curate "our feeds" by following the right people. After Twitter files we see that "the algorithm" is tuned to hide some voices and curate what people talk about. This attacks the notion of "public discourse" - it is heavily moderated by the social networks, with instructions from some institutions of some countries.

I personally think that the use of social networks for "public discourse" is overrated and furthermore that the impact this "public discourse" has on society is way overblown. This book is probably not the place to discuss the usefulness of public discourse for society. Just a few notes – when countries especially in Europe were censoring misinformation and other "hybrid threats", the people instantly moved mostly to Telegram groups. For cypherpunks this is great news – we see that these alternative tools and social networks are discovered and used the moment someone tries to mess with communication. As John Gilmore famously said, "The Net interprets censorship as damage and routes around it". (And I repeat – financial communication is also communication, financial censorship is also censorship – people use cryptocurrencies when states tamper with financial communication using CBDCs or other forms of control).

These regulations of "opinions" and topics of "public discourse" had an effect – they made the communication on forbidden topics **more intense**. (Side note: Please do not use Telegram, it is not end-to-end encrypted).

Some people even realized that opinions (or "truth") should be discovered, not handed down from the leaders.

While mainstream "democratic" folk (i.e., members of current wider establishment) are trying to control the narrative of "public discourse", they also say that it is important for society to have this public discourse. It seems like the minds of people go to the internet to logically argue, discuss and the result of this will be the best solution for society. The common belief is that the politicians would do what the wider society requests – and this request is the result of this mythical "public discourse". But the results are far from correct logical inferences. Some signals are stronger (and not based on merit), some signals are weaker. It **feels** like people are changing the world by chatting on social media, but the impact of these discussions is miniscule. The process is more stochastic, with lots of emergent behavior.

We can look at memetic theory, where membionts are a form of life and they do not prevail and replicate based on merit of the idea, but on how well they can spread using their existing living environment (which is our brains, or if looked at globally – our culture). Is it really that important that someone wins an argument on social media? Does this win last for more than 24 hours? And then someone comes with an insane idea that fits our cultural basis and is spread like crazy. These membionts are formed, they avoid censorship or control like SARS-cov-2 avoided lockdowns. As a form of life, they survive if they adapt to the environment. And the environment is our mass culture and brains of the majority. The immune system is not based on logical refusal of these membionts.

Is this a problem? It would be if it mattered to the ruling society what was the result of yesterday's Twitter fight. It is more layered; opinions are formed across group membership, echoed and politicians basically pick a group or groups that will provide them most votes according to their political rhetoric. There is no "public discourse" that forms the wider governance.

For cypherpunks, this is less important than the other aspects of social networks. Cypherpunks are of course also members of groups, but they are often outside of the traditional political dividing lines. For us, the ideas of most of these mainstream political groups are unacceptable and we must form our own reactions to these pressures (remember, regulation = banning of unapproved behavior, regulation cannot create, only forbid, remove). These reactions are both on an individual level, but also on a group level.

Therefore, groups are of some importance. Not everyone is invited, and shared values are verified at the door. Knowledge is spread to be used in life, not to be used in fights on social networks. We are going back to the roots of private discussions based on topics, as we did with mailing lists and IRC channels.

The acquisition of Twitter by Elon Musk sparked an innovation in public social networks as well. People started to move to Mastodon. Jack Dorsey, the co-founder of Twitter is sponsoring a less centralized alternative called Nostr. These new social networks have either a different algorithm or no algorithm at all. But you can also change it yourself and program it in a way you like. With open-source AI models, you will soon be able to not only filter out the content, but also change the tone of the discussion. Someone writes an angry post and you will only extract the boring facts, if you do not filter it out completely.

Nostr

Nostr is friendly to the Bitcoin Lightning network. The identity is based on a public key, which means it is more difficult to follow people you are interested in – you must learn about their identity somehow. Nostr is a peer-to-peer gossip network with relays. Compared to Mastodon, this means that there is no central banning of instances – if you convince a relay to distribute your messages, you are good to go. The problem might be spam. Messages are free to distribute and there is no cost with spreading them. You can block individual spammers, but creating new keys is almost free. There have been experiments with using Bitcoin Lightning micropayments to incentivize spread and thus fight spam, but this creates a barrier for the masses that will almost instantly kill any network effect.

You can follow me using my key:
npub1m2mvvpjugwdehtaskrcl7ksvdqnnhnjur9v6
g9v266nss504q7mqvlr8p9

Mastodon

Mastodon is older than Nostr and uses a federated model – like e-mail. You create your handle on an instance. This model can fight spam much better. If an instance is spamming, you can block the entire instance and let the instance administrator deal with the user.

The problem is the philosophy of Mastodon that emerged in the network. Many instances are banned because *some* of their users were politically incorrect. Many instances are socialist – they do not like cryptocurrencies, a lot of them ban any form of self-promotion on the instance (self-promotion is in my opinion a better use-case for public social networks than "public discourse"). The hate of cryptocurrencies means that some instances ban whole instances of cryptocurrency users, so people cannot even follow each other.

The legacy social networks

The old big tech social networks feel less useful all the time. Facebook has been almost unusable; the users are getting old – the young generation prefers other social networks. Twitter is often toxic and does not have such a big reach, especially outside of North America. Instagram is not as useful for information gathering. The attention span is shorter and people move to platforms such as TikTok, which is a spyware made in a country that has experience in creating spyware, censorship and information control – China.

I hope that at least among cypherpunks, other social networks (such as Signal, Matrix/Element, P2P IRC, status, Mastodon, Nostr or any other technology that is yet to be discovered) become more important.

Energy production and adaptability

Whatever your opinion on climate change is, we can see how it is handled in society. Transition from fossil fuels to electric vehicles will happen – either by the electric cars becoming a better choice, but more likely by a combination of incentives (such as tax credits) and regulation (banning of sale of fossil fuel vehicles).

What many people do not understand is that aging grids will not be able to handle this load. In Europe, blackouts are not common, the energy companies have found a way to stabilize the grid – matching consumption and production. This balance has a challenge – moving away from fossil fuels to electric vehicles means not only higher load on the grid, but also more volatile demand.

On the other hand, we are moving to less predictable energy production. Moving away from natural gas and in some cases even nuclear to solar and wind means that the production side will be less predictable. What many people do not understand is that production and consumption must match, overproduction is the same problem as underproduction. The sun does not shine at night and the wind does not always blow. The volatility in the production will lead to increased need for predictable and controllable "insurance" products. This can be either natural gas plants, which can be turned on and off on demand, or to the need of vast overproduction and adaptable production processes – like controlling your heating remotely by market actors or turning a Bitcoin miner on and off based on the imbalance in the network, reflected in the spot price.

For us individuals, it might be a good idea to invest in local production. I am not a huge fan of movements towards self-sufficiency and local production in general – I like to make use of comparative advantages and division of labor. Why grow my own food when I am an IT person and I know nothing about farming? I'd rather be a good coder than a bad farmer.

Moving energy production locally might make sense – especially if your livelihood depends on it (and whose does not these days?). First, you save on distribution costs – if you produce your own energy, it does not have to travel hundreds of kilometers. With batteries, you can handle network outages easily. And of course, you basically hedge the price of energy by prepaying the production capital such as solar panels. If there is a chance that the price of energy will go up, it does not concern you. And then it might even make sense to move to electric vehicles, although you need a lot of panels to charge a car, especially in winter in most places on earth.

Some friends that work on cypherpunk energy projects say that access to energy will become the west's version of social credit score. For example, you get your carbon credit allocation and that's how much energy you can use. I am not sure if this will happen, but if energy is important for your livelihood, making your own might make sense.

If you look at broader implications of climate change from the point of view of an individual, what makes sense is to increase adaptability. If you believe climate change (caused by humans or not) is a problem - can you move to a different climate? Do you have air conditioning? Can you run it today? Will you be able to afford it with 3x or 10x energy prices?

A friend of mine told me that buildings are what we build to protect from harsh climates. She lives in Dubai and there is a clear separation of outdoors and indoors. Indoors is what we build to thrive even though outdoors is almost unlivable.

We can do very little against climate change, certainly as individuals. What we can do is to make sure we are adaptable. And one of the best ways to be adaptable is to be wealthy (or at least wealthier). Quitting the fiat world and moving to a parallel economy might help us and others. Cypherpunk strategies might not be mainstream, but they are certainly not exclusive – these options are open for everyone and we do not have to fight for resources, we can all rise in a more abundant future (see 21 millionth of infinity in Cryptocurrencies – Hack your way to a better life).

Home nodes – become your own cloud, bank and credit card company

Cypherpunks are nerds and like to run their software – on home "servers", routers, NAS devices and Raspberry Pi-s laying everywhere all over. We often run our Tor relays, file storage services, Bitcoin and Monero nodes, Lightning nodes, mixers, VPN endpoints and other pieces of software.

I believe these projects will integrate more and you can easily run a Nextcloud alongside your lightning node – of course separated using virtualization with hypervisor or using a project like Qubes.

As I was explaining that people are having bad experiences with banks, the same goes with cloud services. A guy sent a picture of a dermatologic problem near a private area of the child to his wife's phone, who forwarded it to a doctor for consultation and the guy ended up with his Google Fi plan and his Google account cancelled. He could not even call support.

Software authors get kicked out of github for varied reasons. People get kicked out of social networks. In some cases these are legal requirements, such as Russian software developers who cannot be serviced by an American company thanks to embargoes. It is easy to blame Github's owner (Microsoft), but their other option is non-compliance, which would affect their business operations in a big way.

What we must do instead is reject this model altogether. Do we need a company to host our open-source projects? Do we need someone to facilitate sending our photos (and let them look at them and scan them)? Do we need the providers to see what online services we use? Does a (fiat or crypto) bank need to see our transactions and pair them with our identity?

With the rise of projects such as Nextcloud, FreeNAS, or even commercial offerings such as Synology or QNAP, people realize the importance of sovereignty over their data. Cloud services can be used for encrypted data (so the cloud provider does not see what they store), but you also can "run your own cloud". And this is where home nodes come in.

We will hopefully see more projects like Cryptoanarchy Debian Repository (CADR), Umbrel, RaspiBlitz or others.

What to look for in home nodes in the coming years?

- Sharing of files, documents, photos, videos
- "NAS" (Network Attached Storage) functionality for backups with snapshots (which protect against ransomware)
- Online, live document collaboration
- VPN endpoint
- Cryptocurrency nodes and services
  - Lightning wallets with the "Uncle Jim" model of custody – one node with channels per family and friends, yet, people have separate balances. This helps with economies of scale.
  - DeFi infrastructure – monitoring of open trading positions, and margin requirements with notifications.
- Smart home – fire alarms, light control, intelligent thermostat, …

Cryptocurrencies and technical development

Custody and inheritance

For Bitcoin I am looking forward to better solutions for self-custody and inheritance. Not necessarily technological solutions, what would greatly help would be improvements in user experience and simplification. Bitcoin does not have to be for everyone, but it should be for anyone. Anyone, who wants to use it, should be able to use it well – safe, self-sovereign custody is important. I foresee innovations in how the keys are stored and backed-up (for example Trezor T's Shamir Backup was one of the innovations in this area in the past years).

Solutions for safe inheritance without third parties would be great. Bitcoin is over a decade old and I have experienced a few cases of people unexpectedly dying. And they did not leave private keys to their families.

Collateralized loans

Many people find it useful to keep their Bitcoin exposure and at the same time borrow (short) fiat. Current solutions are either custodial, wrap Bitcoin through various bridges on other platforms (WBTC, BTC.b, rBTC) or use centralized exchanges. I have explored this topic quite thoroughly in How to harness the value of Bitcoin without having to sell it e-book and course and Cryptocurrencies book. Bitcoin-native lending protocols or derivative platforms should come in the following years.

One of the projects that I follow and advise is Firefish. It is Bitcoin-native collateralized loans based on very nice security assumptions. Built by bitcoiners for bitcoiners. Hopefully soon with high liquidity, although most providers will probably want KYC. The protocol is open-source. No tokens, only Bitcoin and fiat.

Another interesting project that I co-authored was a paper on Bitcoin-backed derivatives protocol on top of Lightning network. It is a protocol for futures (which can be used as loans – fiat loan is the same as selling spot Bitcoin and buying Bitcoin future), which can be settled off chain, but are enforced using deferred discrete log contracts. DLCs in Lightning channels allow for advanced financial instruments to be provided natively over the lightning network, without any unnecessary on-chain fees.

Wallet usability

What I would like to see is improvements in wallet usability. I think the choices of wallets are already great and there are many options to choose from. Yet there is still much to improve. Integration of NFC protocols, or communicating the payment info using sound rather than QR codes (useful especially in countries where there are feature phones or smartphones that do not have good cameras).

If we look at cryptocurrencies as payment protocol of the Internet, we can integrate the experience. If you pay using payment cards, you do not care which currency you pay in. You choose your payment card provider, you know the fees for interchange and it happens automatically. If you go to a hotel in a foreign country, you do not have to listen to a ten minute talk by the staff on why you should use their preferred fiat coin and not the one that you have. They type the amount, you tap your card and everything happens in the background.

We need this for payments in crypto. You choose a wallet that supports all payment formats. If it is a Bitcoin Lightning wallet and it scans a Monero QR code, there should be no discussion – I do not even need to know what kind of QR code it is. I want to see Bitcoin value, fiat value (depending on what fiat currency I configured) and fees. If the wallet uses some service to do a swap from Lightning to Monero in the background, it does not concern me. If I scan any QR code of a cryptocurrency, the wallet should make the payment happen.

Right now, everyone is shilling their coins. I believe this is a huge waste of energy. If we can economically interact, we should do it without endless discussions about "my coin, your coin". Bitcoin's competition is not Monero, but Visa, Mastercard and USD. Monero is another tool in the network. Same if you are a Monero maximalist.

See The Law of Cryptocurrency Isomorphism (either on my blog or in Cryptocurrencies – Hack your way to a better life)

Bitcoin already has unified QR codes for on-chain and lightning payments. On the seller side, I think it should expand to whatever coins the seller takes (could be a new format similar to LNURL, so it does not have to be embedded in a single dense QR code that is harder to scan). On the wallet side, it should find the cheapest way for the buyer to pay that payment request – look at currencies you have (sorted by preference of spending for example – you want to HODL Bitcoin, not Tether for example), take into account all the fees (network fees, exchange fees, confirmation times) and just find a way to pay it in the best way possible.

We can add additional features, such as PayJoin that increases privacy. Tap to pay (NFC), scan to pay (QR), Bluetooth beacon with matching color code (so you know who you are paying), or sound? All should be supported by good payment systems and some should be supported by the wallets. Let's increase the coverage of how often the payment goes through.

Privacy solutions

I hope that privacy will increase with Bitcoin and other cryptocurrencies. There is quite a lot to do, although we are getting there. One of the most important things is to do it in a way that does not compromise coin usability. While I am glad for solutions based on UTXO mixing, such as Wasabi, Whirlpool or JoinMarket, they have one disadvantage – it is obvious that the person actively mixed the coins. These coins are refused by some services (such as exchanges or even swap services). Also, it is more difficult to explain to the financial police why you mixed the coins, for example in B2B transactions.

For this reason, I prefer solutions where privacy is built-in, for example Monero and Lightning. Monero is a more sophisticated implicit coinjoin, but it is a mandatory feature of every transaction. If a service supports Monero, you know they are OK with coinjoined txs, because there is no other way to make a Monero transaction. Also for business to business transactions, using Monero could be a preferred choice of the counterparty, you can buy it on an exchange legally and you are not doing anything extra fishy – you just pay the invoice using Monero. And the only way to do it is with privacy, that is the only way it works.

For Lightning privacy, I would like to see mainly better onion routing, less public information about channels (does the network really need to know what UTXO backs a channel? Why?) and their balances and better recipient privacy (such as integrating lnproxy to wallets). Lightning is a great privacy tool, it has sender privacy and creates no permanent record of the payment on any blockchain. That also creates forward secrecy – if the node keys leak, they do not help people figure out what payments were through in the past. Imagine a view key to a Monero address leaking – all past transactions are uncovered.

Unbacked (hosted) lightning channels and Liquid / sidechains for easier Lightning adoption

A hosted channel is a channel without on-chain backing. If two nodes agree that they will settle the balance in some other way than an on-chain transaction, it is their choice and it does not decrease the security of the wide lightning network. Routing through a hosted channel is not a problem, because every node that did not agree to this hosted channel will receive a backed payment.

One huge use-case for end-user facing wallets would be to be able to open small channels on sidechains such as Liquid. Because these networks use the same unit of account (Bitcoin) and both support the same lightning implementation (Blockstream's core lightning), creating a hosted channel between a Bitcoin-backed node and Liquid-backed node would unite these networks. This way, lightning can become a layer two solution not only for Bitcoin blockchain, but also for any other compatible chain that uses Bitcoin as a unit of account.

Imagine a consumer wallet such as Phoenix or Breez that can be configured to open channels under let's say 250k sats on Liquid. Yes, it is a comparatively centralized chain, but you can save on fees and the main Bitcoin blockchain would not be bloated as much. Liquid also has confidential transactions, so there would be better privacy. Therefore, receiving sats on Liquid would be cheaper and the channels would confirm fast (although we usually do not need to wait for channel confirmations).

If a wallet has this small channel on liquid, you would still be able to pay any other Lightning invoice – a payment would go from your wallet's channel to the wallet provider and then based on fees through some of the bridges. A bridge would consists of two nodes (operated by the same person/entity), one on liquid and one on bitcoin with an infinite unbacked channel. The bridge nodes would (after this payment goes through) have a higher balance on liquid side and lower balance on bitcoin side, but net balance for the bridge operator would be higher (same amount of bitcoin in channels plus earned fees). The recipient would not see a difference and they would receive sats directly through one of their (bitcoin-backed) channels.

This would greatly increase the capacity of the Lightning network. It would also enable any other compatible side-chain to expand the quantity of lightning channels. I believe this would increase user experience of everyone involved – faster confirmations, better privacy, while keeping users in control (they could flip a switch and open any new channels to Bitcoin, possibly even run a command to consolidate their channels on Liquid into one channel with Bitcoin balance when on-chain fees are low).

This would be especially good for onboarding and showing Lightning to new users, we do not have to spam the main chain, if we only want to send people 5$ to show them how lightning works. And it would seamlessly interoperate with the whole lightning network.

I have written about unbacked channels in 2020.

Note from 2024: Aqua Wallet has a similar approach, but instead of opening channels, they simply do atomic swaps from Lightning to Liquid and vice versa with low fees. This approach also works, although true Lightning would be better and it would expand the network directly.

Asynchronous lightning payments

Lightning adoption on peer-to-peer markets is not taking off as fast as it could. One of the reasons is perceived privacy issues, but one of the drawbacks is a need for the counterparties to be online in a relatively low-latency connection at the time of the payment. If you are paying me to mail you my paperback book, I (or my node) need to be online when you make the payment. It is OK if you order through my server, but if the destination is my mobile wallet, and I am on an airplane, the payment fails. Also, low-latency networks have several privacy issues. If I can reply to a protocol request in 30 minutes, it is much harder to track the connection.

I hope that in 2023 (the sooner the better), technologies for asynchronous payments will be widely implemented in all kinds of nodes (including retail wallets).

Trampolines and automatic lightning channel creation for nodes

Retail wallets do channel management automatically in the background. If I do not have sufficient incoming liquidity, it could be automatically provided to me for a routing fee by a liquidity provider. Being a liquidity provider is the real business model of some lightning wallets that are otherwise Free and Open Source.

Dynamic provision of liquidity needs to be done in a way where payment goes through in any case, but someone must pay for the channel. This is a technological challenge, but for node operators (especially merchants), it could make sense – the sender could pay for channel creation (which incentivizes using existing channels) and the reliability of payments would go up.

There are many technical obstacles. With core lightning for example, you can only have one channel with each node. Retail second generation non-custodial wallets (Phoenix, Breez) do the exact opposite – an end user wallet has many channels with one counterparty node that belongs to the liquidity provider for the wallet. For automatic channel opening, this would have to be the case as well – liquidity providers would open channels automatically, but there would be probably more than one channel with one node. There are other ways to solve this problem. As a node operator, I would like to have an option to manage my channels, but also an option to have automatic on-demand liquidity if someone wants to pay me.

DeFi

Bitcoin-based DeFi

As I mentioned above, I would like to see at least collateralized loans and derivatives built on top of Bitcoin in a decentralized way. Protocols such as firefish or DLC embedded in lightning channels could provide basic utility on the network, without too much bloat on the chain.

There is a lot happening on Bitcoin, but developers often create centralized solutions. We have nice derivative markets, online bets, etc., but they are usually more centralized than their altcoin counterparts.

These are **useful** tools for cypherpunks. They help with keeping your Bitcoin exposure, allow you to short fiat, or reduce risks (hedging).

Better options and other derivatives

While Bitcoin is on the forefront of hard money, HODL usecases and with Lightning it also allows for instant and private payments, altcoins experiment with advanced financial instruments. And they are very useful. For example, options allow you to hedge your collateral risk on collateralized loans. There is currently no way to do decentralized options on Bitcoin – there are theoretical ways, but as I write these lines, there is no market where you can actually buy or sell an option and it will be processed in a decentralized way and backed by Bitcoin collateral.

As crypto markets introduced and popularized novel ideas such as automated market makers using liquidity pools (Uniswap), various stablecoin constructions, which introduced permissionless fiat printing (DAI), and option-like convexity without the need for liquidity for huge option-trees (Squeeth), I think that more innovation will happen outside of Bitcoin. These projects will eventually make it their way back to Bitcoin if they prove useful, but we have to look for the most innovation elsewhere (such as in DarkFi, Ethereum or other ecosystems).

I would personally like to see more decentralized options and option-like products (such as Squeeth alternative for Bitcoin), synthetic assets (synthetic shares of companies or commodities without KYC) and prediction markets.

Prediction markets are built on Bitcoin in a semi-centralized way, but they often limit questions to topics (such as sports and politics) or do content moderation. Solving permissionless, easy to use, liquid prediction markets that use real money would be really useful for society. Read more in Prediction markets – crowdsourcing information for good decisions in Cryptocurrencies – Hack your way to a better life, or on my blog.

Personal development, education, voluntaryist parenting, biohacking, mindfulness, …

There is this archetype of a cypherpunk that drinks sugary energy drinks, eats microwaved frozen pizza, smokes joints and does not sleep – ever. This archetypal cypherpunk does not leave their home, does not date, is antisocial and does not have kids.

In my experience, most cypherpunks are very far from this archetype. They want to live a high quality life. They exercise, implement biohacking for higher energy, fine-tune their sleep, meditate daily in order to be able to focus better and understand themselves better. They focus on personal development. They date and when they have kids, they try to implement a parenting style and educational style that is compatible with their world-view, such as non-violent communication (NVC), voluntaryist parenting and unschooling.

These topics are personal and everyone is at a different phase of their lives, trying to focus on different aspects of self-improvement. The reason I included this part is to let you know that this is available and other cypherpunks are doing it too. We are all humans (even though some of us are cyborgs and we are all somehow interconnected with machines) and we strive to be better. Most ideologies rely on changing other people in order to achieve their goals. We only have to change ourselves and consciously choose our peers. Becoming a better person ourselves, creating better, loving families is beautiful for its own sake, but it leads to a better society. We do not have to wait for it though, it is already available.

Conclusion

This book is a look at my expectations of the next few years of development – what I am looking for. I do not intend to predict what will happen so much as identify current needs of cypherpunks and hope that there are enough incentives for entrepreneurs to provide solutions to these problems. For some predictions, it might take longer (such as open-source multi-trillion parameter neural networks). Many might not happen, or a better solution than I propose will be found. I hope that this book describes at least partially the future we are heading to. Alternatively, the future might be even a little bit better!

I do not mean to be overly optimistic, but the timeframe 2023-2025 was chosen consciously. We overestimate what we can do in three months, but underestimate what we can do in three years.

I believe we will see a lot of growth in the coming years!

Not all the seeds
have taken hold... But
look at the beauty!